LYDIA RUANNA

Sandstorm

A Collection of Poetry

To my past self

This too shall pass

Table of Contents

Acknowledgements

Thank you to every man I have loved or have thought about loving. Each and every poem is a lesson from one or several of you.

Thank you to the first for inspiring the poem that titled this book.

Thank you to the last for inspiring me to write again and supporting me through the process.

Thank you to all of the friends who offered to give me heartfelt feedback. It was incredibly validating to see my poems have the desired effect on you.

Thank you to Niokoba, who designed the cover, layout, and illustrations shown in this edition of the book.

Thank you to my past self, for never giving up.

Introduction

Bumblebees

I think we are all like bumblebees;
fumbling around,
looking for a place to land.

Dating

His Utterance

I can talk about love
All I want
In as poetic a manner
As pleases me
But
I will not feel certain
Until he says the word to me
In a chain of three

Moonshout

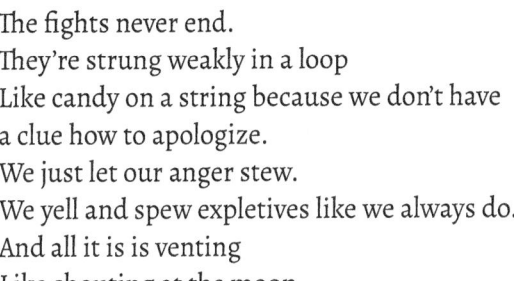

The fights never end.
They're strung weakly in a loop
Like candy on a string because we don't have
a clue how to apologize.
We just let our anger stew.
We yell and spew expletives like we always do.
And all it is is venting
Like shouting at the moon.

Eventually you march upstairs
With no more than your heart laid bare
You've got nothing to show for it
No lessons learned
To you it all seems unfair.

When you come downstairs
You pretend to forget what was shared

Someday the string will break
The moon will shout back
Heaven will shake from the weight of
the mess that we make.

Racehorse

A hike in the snow
So tired
In pain
You wear snowshoes and walk away
They call you a race horse but I am no longer the rider
And you are no longer tame

No Fortune Today

Decorations splayed
"Do you care about Valentine's Day?"
Restaurants can be busy
But we can still celebrate

Chinese takout. I pay.
We eat on bins and crates
No brown sauce on my plate
You won't share your entree

Hunger pangs

But I beg for you to stay
Scratchy lingerie
An unused condom
Thrown away

Cookie has no fortune today

I Won't Say No

Asexual tendencies
Uncomfortable around anything
With a brain below the belt
But exceptions come with everything
And that is my tell
Allowing him to sit a little closer
To myself

Erode

My heart of stone
Your eyes of water
Calming, terrifying

My heart and I will sit here
And let you grind me down
Until all the little pieces of who I am
Retreat into your sea
And drown

Drunk on your eyes
As the salt stings mine

Lion's Pain

Am I supposed to be the one
To fix their shallow soul?
Or should I walk away?

And how does one judge the depths of one's soul
Without getting too close
And becoming prey?

The Void

I speak into a dark abyss
Try to shed some light on it
But all there is
Is endless silence

My voice echoes
Lost and listless
Desperation thickens
I beg you to listen

How long will your punishment last
This jail of quietude
Your condemnation eats at me
Endless solitude

You lack the vindication
To grant me pardon
You hold your grudges
in your dark garden

Time to take out my shovel
And dig myself a hole
Because even hell is lighter
than your cursed soul

Lost

Trying to dissect it all
Identify where things went wrong
The autopsy's been stalled
I keep thinking it's my fault

I spent too many sleepless nights on you

Play Fair

It's funny
They ask you to come
Say it will be fun
But precisely when you arrive
They run

Values

Fastened to my values;
Controlled by my need
To understand you.
Failure is fatigue.

Embers

Lingering feelings
And an untethered soul
I need a paperweight to hold me down

Smoking in fire
Burning like coal
I wish for the soft cold ground

But I stand on the embers
Stubborn, unmoving
I must not rely on you

Siri

Hey Siri,
How do I keep walls up
When I'm the one
Tearing them down?

Let Me See

I just want a little peek
Cracked and squinted
One eye open
Blurred vision
Peripherally
Just once
Give me a piece of your mind

Hypochondriac

It starts as a ringing in your ears
A headache or some other clue
Like hypochondriacs
I've been known to assume
That if I think it
It must be true

Maybe I love you

Lydia Ruanna

Breaking

Silence

I was told I was amazing
Perfect
Golden
But eventually
They ran out of words
They opted for silence
Now I am nothing at all

Sticky

So sticky.
I can't get rid of the way
You touched me like I was yours
Like honey dripping from my hands.
You treated me like I was everything
And it felt so real.
It sticks with me.

No More Hope

When he wants you,
He is everything you need.
He can't say no;
All he does is appease.

When he loses all hope,
He's a ghost.
I don't know him anymore;
He's a hoax

The Easiest Goodbye

Of all the relationships I have had,
Ours was the quickest to get over,
Because I was grieving
In it.
Tears on my pillow,
Silent in the night,
I grieved every day;
That is how I got by.
And when it finally ended,
I was relieved.
That's how I got over you.

Puzzler

The last guy was a talker
Said smooth, wonderful things
But this one, he's a walker
A thinker
Always puzzling

We said our goodbyes for the summer
He was working, I told myself
Every silent night a bummer
Puzzle stuck up on the shelf

I wanted to leave him alone
But anxiety was creeping
When I reached for the puzzle
Something was missing

No picture to guide me
Light to the touch
Open it up
No pieces, had a hunch

When I saw him in the fall
I still held hope for us
I said we could be friends
Didn't want it to end
It's not something my therapist
Recommends

She holds your puzzle now
Thinks she can figure you out
I'd love to believe her but I have my doubts

Maybe
Stop giving your puzzle to others
Figure yourself out.

His Currency

His shining weapon, his true sorcery
Was his affinity towards opportunity
Every kind deed was a penny of his currency
A month of friendship worth a night of lust

He was a salesman in coercion
Convincing me to give in to these sexual favors
A printed page
An opened jar
A ride home in the dark

His weapon rusted
His magic faded
Investments failed
Eroded trust
Our friendship faded into dust

My Life

I see all the different paths of my life;
All the forks in the road.
I don't see one that makes me more happy than the rest.

I see paths that may take some getting used to,
Paths that will require pain and growth;
A sense of achievement,
A sense of hope.

I see easy paths
Where people follow me, worship me,
Love me for what they think I am.

I see the golden path
Where he loves me for who I am.

A multitude of timelines
And a million include him.
In some he loves me
And in some as just a friend.

In some he worships me
In some he sees my flaws
In some he tries to help me heal
In some he digs his claws

In some I see him find true love
In some I see him fall

And somehow my paths become all about him;
His life, his love, his death and all.

Colder

He dressed me up in flattering phrases,
Calling me smart and kind and worthy of love
Before trying to undress me and leaving me
Colder
Older
Wondering if I should dress myself for once

Casual

If I knew you were destined to leave I wouldn't have loved you
And perhaps I didn't love you as much as I loved the idea of you.
But it hurts me to think that your idea of me was
Laying in your bed casually.
Maybe I should measure my expectations accordingly.

Pessimist

Pessimists sit with you in the dark
And bleed light from your soul
Each time you dim
They slice once more
Now both of you sit in the dark
Cold

Overanalyzing

I will continue to read
And reread
Every inch of this book
Until I find the part
Where you stopped loving me

Timelines

I told him I loved him and drove away
Now everytime I drive I cry
I hear the word love and my eyes shimmer
I grieve for another timeline

Don't worry
I'll be fine

Not Sure Anymore

Desired and unwanted
Secret meetings and progress halted
Red flags faded pink
Just happy to be sipped like a drink

But tossed away so easily
Ignored like faded ink

How many tears
Over the years I've shed
Convinced the only way to be in love
Is to be in bed

Silver Bullet

I could not dodge his bullet
It is lodged in my heart
Each beat tears it further apart
Until it is a broken bleeding mess and he
Departs

Time to restart

Learning

Ashes

Dynasties will fall before
I admit my faults.
They'll be awaiting my confession
Until the sun falls.
Fire and fury
Ashes and all I know is
I'm not wrong.

Breakaway

I am breaking the 4th wall
I am not putting up with your shit anymore
I am leaving this life that was destined for me,
And carving out my own reality

Lumberjack

There are splinters in the cracks
Fingertips feel for smooth grooves
I am feeling like a lumberjack
Bringing my ax back
And letting it split through you

Sea of Thieves

I'm tired of chasing a dream
Looking for love in a sea of thieves
Desensitized to all the things
They say to get inside of me

Testing boundaries
Convincing
Pleading
Molding every thought in my head

Creeping ever closer to an edge

I feel them splashing softly
Corroding my metal beams
Slowly chipping away
At my integrity

I'm tired of trying to appease
I will not bend to the sea of thieves

I'd rather sink
As one to admire
Than as an object
Of desire

Royalty

Every time you leave I bleed
And the space it creates in my veins
Makes way for blue blood
I become royalty
My crown is bloodstained
This is a new reign
Of loyalty

June Bugs

I've improved. I see red flags easily now. I pick them out like constellations in the night sky. I point them out like june bugs or faces in clouds. I feel so satisfied.

What I still have trouble with, though, is my habit of tearing flags down before anyone can see them and pretending they were never there. I push them down when they bounce back up and drown them in white flags, hoping the heat will fade them pink so that all of my efforts will make sense, finally.

I Am Sand

We walked for days
My feet were tired
He asked for mountain tops
I gave him what he desires
Too scared to tell him I want beach sand
Too scared his dreams are more grand than my hand.

Finally I stand
He lets go
I am sand
And he wants snow

Rocky Shore

I showed you the sun
Held your hand and led you to a rocky shore
We sat staring out at the vastness I adore
I was happy then, to my core

But just as rain began to pour
your feet became torn
Shells bit them bare
as you ran from the shore

Oh, baby
When you run from storms
The sun is no longer yours
To adore

Run Away

Narcissism is shifting blame
Underestimating pain
Always deflecting complaints
And making you feel insane

Bathing in their vanity
Floating in their apathy
So they won't feel alone
In their insanity

Quickly now
Run away
Casually

Craving

I no longer ache to be told things
I already know

I no longer crave your touch
I do not starve myself of my own

Teaching Nomad

Do not trick yourself into believing that you will teach them something, that after they have had their epiphany you can come back and welcome them home; accept their apologies and stop feeling alone.

No.

The reality is that you are a teaching nomad, and your lesson will not reach them until they are long gone. They aren't sorry for how they acted. Heck, they probably don't even remember. They are just sorry you had the sense to leave. Are you going to apologize for that?

Don't come back.

Nostalgia

Today

I remembered your birthday today.
I didn't want to.
It just happened.

Just like I did on
Graduation day
Just like I did
When I left Maine
Just like I did
When Covid hit

Never a year missed

I remember the movies
Our first date
I remember the bear
On Valentine's Day
I remember the van
When things felt gray
Texting you the words
Stable, unafraid
When you broke up with me
And I just walked away

You were my first everything
What more can I say?
I still wish you a
Happy birthday.

Sandstorm

He has a piece of my heart, like all the rest.
My words feel like dust in the wind to him.
Maybe one day
I'll be a sandstorm.

Moments

Despite everything you've done
The damage and the pain
I still miss those little moments of happiness
Striking rarely
Like lightning in the rain

Borrowed Grief

I used to fill whole notebooks of you
It felt like I was felling trees
Whole forests were falling down, grieving you.
Smashed and pulped and bleeding for you
Glued and bleached and cut to size
Bound and wrapped and shipped for me to coat
in tears caused by your lies
I've said my goodbyes

Nostalgia

He was nostalgia;
A dark and artful masterpiece painted
In long and wistful strokes
Of charm and smarts and capability
With secrets interloped.

Off to the side,
Lighter strokes reside,
Mixing with red and blue.

Not sure what to do,
White accepts brighter hues.

His darker strokes reveal darker meanings:
Coercive and cunning and sneaking.
His figure seems to be drinking in white as it
Slips closer
Sinking

When the painting is done it is clear to see;
His anger and sadness emanating
Rays of purple grasp for the hands of the white willow wisp
That is me
It's always so easy to see when they leave.

Alchemy

Touching him was alchemy.

I touched every part
He hated about himself
And loved with all of my heart.

Even when doing so
tore myself apart

His skin remains gold
Despite the fact
That I lost hold long ago.

It was around the time I realized
Under the skin
There was mold

Ripped Up Tires

I saw ripped up tires on the highway
It made me think of you
How we crashed and burned
Like we always do

Our hearts shredded
And left behind

Just rubble and ashes
I passed right by

Reminded of you
And every other man
I've fallen into

Honesty

In the end I forgave him
Everything he ever said to me was honest

And true

And resenting him for honesty meant
I was willing to accept deceit.

And deceit has left me far more broken than truth.

Laughing

She was all over you
I remember it clearly
Because even though I didn't know you
I thought of you dearly
We all laughed
But she laughed louder

The One

Caution

Waves,
Oscillations;
Back and forth,
Up and down;

Times of happiness,
Times of doubt;

A rocky bottom,
A glass ceiling,
And the vast space in between,

Fuels caution,
Measured footsteps,
And hope for a new beginning.

I am the Tide

If I am the tide
You are the moon
Your gravity
Pulls me
Closer to you
I run away
Then back to you

Every
Single
Night

Meant To Be

I wondered why it was taking so long
Banged my head on a wall
Wondered what was wrong with me
Wondered if it was even meant to be
Pondered solemnly
The idea of being alone for all eternity

The wall has chipped and cracked
A light shines through
And though it wasn't necessary
I know all my suffering led me to you

His Name is Church

Every morning there is a cat on my chest
But it's cold and has its teeth bared
The sunrise leaves shadows where you should be
Reminders of what we shared

And as the morning fades
Your shadow burns away like L.A. fog
Pretending it never happened at all

But every night there is a cat on my chest
A warm and purring weighted blanket
And every night I get a good rest
Because you haven't left me yet

Tea Time

Anxiety is a curse for me
A self-fulfilling prophecy
If we ever have an anniversary
It will be a miracle

I've healed my mind
But some scars run deep
So give it time
Tea tastes better steeped.

Breaking the Silence

He said I was perfect
And funny
And nice
And he said those things
For the rest of his life

Happily

Straining to see
Blurry and unsure
Wobbly
Torture

These men don't know what they are looking for
They just want something warm
They want a mother figure
In a younger form

Someone to tell them they're great
When they haven't done anything
Someone to serve their favorite foods
Someone to serve them

Happily

Easy on the eyes
Crisp and clear
Steady
My dear

These men don't know what they're looking for
But you do
You know

Your actions tell me you love me
Your words echo the same
Because all you want is to be loved
A break from all the pain

And I serve you because you serve me
We are equal and whole
We complement each other
We bend and fold

And we serve

Happily

Hazel

When I ask you what color my eyes are
You'll say "I'm not sure"
And when I ask my mom
She'll say
"Brown like mine!"
But when I ask him he laughs
"They're so much more than that.
A mahogany center blending into green,
A speck in the corner,
A rim of evergreen,
And the spark in the middle
Whenever you see me."

Paramour

I've looked into the eyes of men and judged
their souls before
But never as more than a paramour

Their gaze averted, avoiding my core
Leaving me always yearning for more
Stuck in the shallows of the pool floor
Rusting, crumbling, paramour

But I'm spoiled now
This ocean runs deep
Polished and dark
I take an abyssal leap

With you I feel so adored
Never again tortured